A Journey into Indian Mentality

C. P. Kumar
Reiki Healer & Author
Roorkee - 247667, India

Disclaimer

While every effort has been made to ensure the accuracy and completeness of the content in this book, the author cannot guarantee that the information contained herein is error-free, up-to-date, or suitable for every individual circumstance.

The author shall not be held liable or responsible for any errors or omissions in the content of the book, nor for any damages, or losses that may arise from any actions taken based upon the suggestions or contents presented in the book.

Readers are advised to use their own judgment and discretion in applying the information provided in this book, and to consult with qualified professionals before taking any action based on the contents of this book. The author disclaims any and all liability or responsibility for any actions taken or not taken based on the information contained in this book.

DEDICATION

To the vibrant tapestry of Indian culture, history, and society, this book is dedicated. It is an exploration into the intricate and multifaceted facets of Indian mentality, an ode to the diverse and evolving mindset that has shaped generations.

To the countless individuals whose lives have been woven into the fabric of family dynamics and the joint family system, this dedication extends. May the understanding of these connections deepen, fostering appreciation for the ties that bind and the impact they have on the unfolding stories of each individual.

In recognition of the ongoing journey towards gender equality, this book is dedicated to those challenging traditional gender roles and expectations. May this exploration contribute to the dialogue surrounding the challenges faced by different genders in Indian society.

To the rich tapestry of caste and social hierarchy, this dedication is made. May the examination of historical contexts and contemporary impacts lead to a deeper understanding of the complexities surrounding social structures and individual lives.

To the omnipresence of religion in daily life, this dedication extends. Through the exploration of rituals, festivals, and daily practices, may a greater understanding of the profound influence of spirituality on the Indian mentality emerge.

To the myriad expressions of love and partnership, this dedication is offered. May the insights into the cultural nuances surrounding marriage and matrimony contribute to a more nuanced understanding of the evolving concepts of partnerships in India.

To the influence of tradition on personal choices, this book is dedicated. May the exploration of how traditional values shape decisions related to marriage, lifestyle, and self-identity shed light on the intricate balance between heritage and modernity.

To the pursuit of education and career, this dedication is made. May the analysis of the Indian approach to these pursuits contribute to a deeper understanding of the significance of professional success in shaping the Indian mindset.

To the entrepreneurial spirit and business culture, this dedication extends. May the overview of entrepreneurship in India and the role of family in business enterprises shed light on the dynamic intersection of tradition and innovation.

To the diverse landscape of media and entertainment preferences, this book is dedicated. May the exploration of the Indian psyche surrounding media consumption and entertainment choices illuminate the impact of Bollywood and regional cinema on the collective imagination.

To the political awareness and civic engagement of Indians, this dedication is offered. May the analysis of how politics influences everyday life foster a greater understanding of the role individuals play in shaping their society.

To the intricate web of social expectations and relationships, this book is dedicated. May the examination of societal expectations regarding friendships, community involvement, and social networks contribute to a deeper appreciation of the interconnectedness of Indian lives.

To the interplay between modernization, globalization, and traditional values, this dedication is made. May the exploration of these influences shed light on the dynamic nature of the Indian mentality in the face of evolving global dynamics.

To the spiritual seekers and mindfulness practitioners, this book is dedicated. May the exploration of spirituality in the Indian mindset, including meditation practices, yoga, and the quest for inner peace, inspire a deeper connection with the spiritual dimensions of life.

To the resilience demonstrated in the face of crises and challenges, this dedication extends. May the examination of how the Indian mentality copes with adversity inspire strength and fortitude in the face of life's uncertainties.

To the younger generations reshaping traditional values, this book is dedicated. May the analysis of generational shifts and changing values inspire a forward-looking perspective that embraces progress while honoring the wisdom of the past.

To the unfolding chapters of the future, this dedication is made. May the speculation on how the Indian mentality might evolve in the face of ongoing social, economic, and technological changes serve as a compass for navigating the uncharted waters that lie ahead.

C. P. Kumar

CONTENTS

PREFACE

Embarking on a journey into the intricate tapestry of Indian mentality is akin to navigating a labyrinth of diverse cultures, rich history, and societal intricacies. This exploration is not merely an academic exercise but an attempt to unravel the essence of what shapes the collective consciousness of a nation that has stood the test of time. "A Journey into Indian Mentality" delves into the multifaceted layers that contribute to the unique mindset of India, a nation where tradition seamlessly coexists with the modern, and where the past intricately weaves itself into the fabric of the present.

In the introductory chapters, we navigate the historical currents that have shaped the Indian psyche, understanding the profound influence of cultural, societal, and historical factors. As we traverse the pages of this book, we encounter the cornerstone of Indian society - the family. The joint family system, deeply rooted in tradition, becomes a focal point as we explore the dynamics of familial ties and their profound impact on individuals' lives.

Gender roles, an ever-evolving landscape, are scrutinized, revealing the complexities of traditional expectations and the challenges faced by different genders in contemporary Indian society. Moving forward, the book unravels the intricate layers of the caste system, examining its historical roots and contemporary implications on social structures and individual destinies.

Religion, a pervasive force, is explored in its various dimensions - from the rituals woven into daily life to the celebration of festivals that mark the Indian calendar. We navigate through the intricate maze of marriage and matrimony, understanding the cultural nuances that surround arranged and love marriages and the evolving concepts of partnerships.

Tradition emerges as a guiding force in personal choices, influencing decisions related to marriage, lifestyle, and self-identity. Education and career pursuits are scrutinized, offering an analysis of the Indian approach to education and the significance of professional success. Entrepreneurship and business culture, deeply embedded in familial ties, are presented as key elements in understanding the economic landscape.

As we delve into the psyche of the Indian populace, we examine their media and entertainment preferences, uncovering the impact of Bollywood and regional cinema on shaping cultural narratives. Political awareness, civic engagement, and the pervasive influence of politics on daily life are analyzed, providing insights into the role of governance in shaping societal norms.

Social expectations, relationships, and community involvement are explored, offering a glimpse into the intricate web of societal connections. The book then turns its gaze towards the impact of modernization and globalization on traditional values, dissecting the delicate balance between progress and preservation.

Spirituality and mindfulness emerge as integral components of the Indian mentality, with chapters dedicated to understanding meditation practices, yoga, and the quest for inner peace. The resilience demonstrated in the face of crises and challenges is scrutinized, offering a glimpse into the indomitable spirit that defines the Indian mentality.

As we navigate through the pages, we witness the ebb and flow of generational shifts, analyzing how younger generations are reshaping traditional values and adopting more progressive perspectives. Finally, the book ventures into the speculative terrain, pondering on the future of Indian mentality amidst ongoing social, economic, and technological changes.

This journey into Indian mentality is not a static exploration; it is a dynamic odyssey that unfolds across the chapters, revealing a nation in constant flux, embracing the duality of tradition and modernity. As readers embark on this journey, they are invited to witness the complexities, contradictions, and harmonies that shape the soul of India.

C. P. Kumar
Reiki Healer & Author
Former Scientist 'G', National Institute of Hydrology
Roorkee - 247667, India
Web: https://www.angelfire.com/nh/cpkumar/virgo.html

Chapter 1. Introduction to Indian Mentality

India, a land of diverse landscapes, languages, and traditions, is also a tapestry of rich mentalities that have evolved over millennia. To embark on a journey into the Indian mentality is to traverse a complex terrain shaped by a confluence of cultural, historical, and societal factors. This chapter serves as a gateway into understanding the multifaceted aspects of the Indian mindset, exploring the intricate web of influences that sculpt thoughts, actions, and perspectives.

Cultural Mosaic: The Foundation of Indian Mentality

1. Diversity in Unity

India's cultural richness is exemplified by its ability to seamlessly integrate diverse traditions, languages, and belief systems. The Indian mentality draws strength from this mosaic of cultures, creating a unique tapestry where unity is found in diversity. From the snow-capped peaks of the Himalayas to the sun-drenched shores of Kerala, each region contributes distinct flavors to the collective consciousness, fostering a mentality that accommodates a spectrum of perspectives.

2. Spirituality and Philosophy

At the core of the Indian mentality lies a deep-rooted connection with spirituality and philosophy. Ancient texts such as the Vedas and Upanishads have provided a philosophical foundation that continues to influence contemporary thought. Concepts like dharma (righteous duty) and karma (action and consequence) shape the moral compass of individuals, contributing to a mindset that often seeks a harmonious coexistence with the universe.

Historical Echoes: Shaping the Indian Psyche

1. Ancient Civilizations and Empires

India's history is a tapestry woven with the threads of ancient civilizations like the Indus Valley and the Mauryan and Gupta Empires. The echoes of these eras resonate in the collective memory, influencing the Indian mentality. From the emphasis on education during the Gupta period to the administrative prowess of the Mauryas, historical legacies continue to shape contemporary attitudes toward knowledge, governance, and societal structures.

2. Colonial Impact

The arrival of European powers, particularly the British, left an indelible mark on the Indian psyche. Colonial rule not only altered political landscapes but also influenced social dynamics and perceptions of self-worth. The struggle for independence, led by figures like Mahatma Gandhi, injected a sense of resilience and collective identity into the Indian mentality. The scars of colonization continue to influence perceptions of power, authority, and national pride.

Societal Undercurrents: Modern Realities

1. Caste System and Social Hierarchies

The caste system, deeply ingrained in Indian society for centuries, has significantly impacted the collective mindset. While efforts have been made to address caste-based discrimination, its historical influence continues to shape social dynamics. Understanding the nuances of caste-related mentalities is crucial to grasping the complexities within Indian society and the ongoing quest for social justice.

2. Family and Community Bonds

The Indian mentality places a strong emphasis on familial and community ties. Extended families often coexist harmoniously, with relationships extending beyond immediate kin. This interconnectedness contributes to a collective mindset where the well-being of the family and community is paramount. Exploring the dynamics of these relationships provides insights into the values that guide individual choices and societal structures.

Modern Influences: Globalization and Urbanization

1. Economic Shifts and Ambitions

As India undergoes rapid economic development, aspirations and ambitions are evolving. The pursuit of success in the global arena is reshaping the Indian mentality, introducing elements of competition, innovation, and individualism. Understanding the intersection of traditional values and modern aspirations is crucial in deciphering the current state of the Indian mindset.

2. Media and Technology

In an era dominated by technology and media, the Indian mentality is exposed to a myriad of influences. The impact of social media, television, and the internet on shaping opinions and perceptions cannot be understated. Analyzing how these mediums contribute to the formation of mentalities and attitudes provides a glimpse into the evolving nature of the Indian mindset in the 21st century.

Challenges and Opportunities

1. Navigating Cultural Sensitivities

As the world becomes increasingly interconnected, navigating the Indian mentality requires an appreciation for cultural sensitivities. Respect for traditions, customs, and diverse perspectives is essential for meaningful engagement. Sensitivity to regional variations and an understanding of the historical context can foster more profound connections and partnerships.

2. Embracing Change and Continuity

The Indian mentality is in a state of flux, balancing the forces of tradition and modernity. Embracing this duality is crucial for individuals and organizations seeking to navigate the Indian landscape. Recognizing the resilience embedded in the Indian mindset allows for a more nuanced understanding, enabling fruitful collaborations and interactions.

Conclusion: Unraveling the Tapestry

Embarking on a journey into the Indian mentality is akin to unraveling a tapestry woven with threads of tradition, history, and contemporary influences. The interplay of cultural, historical, and societal factors creates a dynamic mindset that is both resilient and adaptable. As we delve deeper into subsequent chapters, we will explore specific facets of the Indian mentality, unveiling the layers that contribute to its richness and complexity. In doing so, we hope to foster a deeper understanding of the diverse mental landscapes that shape the vibrant mosaic of India.

Introduction

The fabric of Indian society is intricately woven with the threads of family values and traditions. At the heart of this societal structure lies the joint family system, an age-old institution that has shaped the lives of generations. This article explores the profound impact of family dynamics and the joint family system on individuals, delving into the core principles that underpin this unique aspect of Indian mentality.

Understanding the Importance of Family Ties

Family, in the Indian context, is not merely a social unit; it is a sacred institution that forms the foundation of an individual's identity and values. The concept of family extends beyond the nuclear unit to encompass a broader network of relatives, creating a support system that transcends generations. This emphasis on familial ties is deeply rooted in cultural, religious, and historical traditions.

1. Cultural Significance

India's diverse cultural landscape is reflected in the myriad ways families express their values. Whether through rituals, festivals, or daily practices, families play a pivotal role in preserving and passing on cultural heritage. The joint family system, in particular, becomes a vessel for the transmission of these cultural nuances, fostering a sense of belonging and continuity.

2. Religious Influence

Many Indian religions emphasize the sanctity of family life. The joint family system finds resonance in religious scriptures, which often extol the virtues of living harmoniously with extended family members. This religious backing further solidifies the importance of family ties in the minds of individuals, shaping their mentality and worldview.

3. Historical Perspective

The joint family system has deep historical roots, tracing back centuries. It evolved as a practical response to the socio-economic demands of agrarian societies, where multiple generations lived and worked together to ensure the family's survival. This historical context continues to influence the perception of family in modern India.

The Joint Family System

The joint family system, or "sanyukt parivaar", is a distinctive feature of Indian society, where multiple generations coexist under one roof. This system has its own set of principles and dynamics that contribute to the holistic development of individuals within the family structure.

1. Collective Decision-Making

One of the defining characteristics of the joint family system is the collective decision-making process. Important family matters are discussed and decided upon by the elders, taking into account the opinions of every member. This fosters a sense of unity and shared responsibility, reinforcing the idea that the family is a cohesive unit.

2. Economic Interdependence

In a joint family, members often share economic resources and responsibilities. The pooling of financial resources ensures that the family collectively faces challenges and enjoys successes. This economic interdependence strengthens familial bonds and teaches individuals the value of cooperation and mutual support.

3. Role of Elders

Elders hold a central position in the joint family structure, serving as repositories of wisdom and experience. Their guidance and advice shape the values and behaviors of younger family members. The respect accorded to elders fosters a sense of continuity and tradition, grounding individuals in a cultural framework.

Impact on Individuals' Lives

The joint family system leaves an indelible mark on the lives of those who grow up within its embrace. While it offers a supportive environment, it also presents challenges and opportunities that significantly shape the mentalities of individuals.

1. Sense of Belonging

Growing up in a joint family instills a profound sense of belonging. The constant presence of relatives, the shared rituals, and the collective celebrations create a familial bond that goes beyond mere blood ties. This sense of belonging provides individuals with a strong emotional foundation, impacting their self-esteem and mental well-being.

2. Social Skills and Cooperation

Interacting with a diverse group of family members in a joint family setting hones social skills and teaches the importance of cooperation. Individuals learn to navigate complex relationships, resolve conflicts, and collaborate for the greater good of the family. These skills become invaluable assets in the broader societal context.

3. Cultural Identity and Tradition

The joint family system serves as a crucible for the preservation of cultural identity and tradition. From the observance of religious rituals to the celebration of festivals, individuals imbibe cultural values that become an integral part of their identity. This cultural richness shapes their worldview and influences their decisions and actions.

Challenges and Evolution of the Joint Family System

While the joint family system has been a cornerstone of Indian mentality, it is not without its challenges. Changing societal dynamics, economic pressures, and evolving individual aspirations have led to a gradual shift in the prevalence of nuclear families. Understanding these challenges is crucial for comprehending the nuanced interplay between tradition and modernity in Indian family dynamics.

1. Economic Pressures

In a rapidly changing economic landscape, the traditional joint family system can face challenges in sustaining itself. The need for individual economic independence often prompts family members to explore opportunities outside the joint family structure, leading to a gradual disintegration of the traditional model.

2. Individual Aspirations

The aspirations of the younger generation are evolving, with an increasing emphasis on personal goals and career pursuits. This shift can sometimes clash with the collective ethos of the joint family system, as individuals seek autonomy and the freedom to make independent choices.

3. Changing Social Dynamics

Urbanization and globalization have brought about significant changes in social dynamics. The joint family system, rooted in agrarian societies, may find it challenging to adapt to the fast-paced, individualistic nature of modern urban life. As a result, nuclear families are becoming more prevalent in urban areas.

Conclusion

Family dynamics and the joint family system are integral aspects of the Indian mentality, shaping the values, behaviors, and identities of individuals. Understanding the significance of family ties and the intricate web of relationships within a joint family provides insights into the rich tapestry of Indian culture. While the joint family system faces challenges in the modern era, its enduring impact on individuals cannot be understated. As India continues its journey into the future, the interplay between tradition and change in family dynamics will continue to shape the collective psyche of the nation.

Chapter 3. Gender Roles and Expectations

Introduction

In the kaleidoscope of Indian culture, gender roles and expectations have long played a defining role in shaping societal norms and individual identities. Rooted in tradition and influenced by historical, religious, and cultural factors, these roles have undergone a fascinating evolution. This article delves into the multifaceted landscape of gender roles in India, exploring the intricacies of traditional expectations, the evolving dynamics, and the challenges faced by different genders in this diverse and complex society.

Traditional Gender Roles in India

1. Historical Context: The Foundations of Gender Roles

To comprehend contemporary gender roles in India, one must trace their roots to ancient scriptures and societal structures. The Manusmriti, an ancient Hindu legal text, delineated specific roles for men and women, setting the groundwork for traditional expectations. Women were assigned the role of homemakers, while men were deemed providers and protectors.

2. Family Dynamics: The Pillars of Tradition

The family, a cornerstone of Indian society, has historically been a microcosm of traditional gender roles. Women were expected to adhere to notions of modesty, sacrifice, and devotion, while men were burdened with the responsibility of familial welfare and social standing. These roles, often rigid and hierarchical, permeated every aspect of life.

3. Religious Influence: Goddesses and Social Constructs

Paradoxically, the rich tapestry of Indian mythology features powerful goddesses embodying strength and independence. Yet, societal structures tended to restrict women to more conventional roles. The interplay between religious ideals and social constructs created a complex web of expectations, contributing to the enduring dichotomy in gender roles.

Evolving Gender Dynamics in Modern India

1. Education: Empowering Minds and Breaking Barriers

The winds of change began to blow with the advent of education. As literacy rates rose, especially among women, there emerged a gradual shift in perceptions. Education became a catalyst for dismantling stereotypes, empowering women to challenge traditional roles and aspire to careers beyond the domestic sphere.

2. Economic Independence: Redefining Power Dynamics

The economic landscape of India witnessed a transformation with women actively participating in the workforce. This shift not only redefined financial independence but also challenged preconceived notions about a woman's role in society. The notion of a sole male breadwinner started to give way to a more equitable distribution of responsibilities.

3. Urbanization and Globalization: Catalysts of Change

The rapid urbanization and globalization of India brought with them exposure to diverse cultures and perspectives.

This exposure led to a questioning of traditional gender norms, creating a space for individuals to explore identities outside the confines of prescribed roles. Cities became crucibles of change, fostering a more inclusive and progressive mindset.

Challenges Faced by Different Genders

1. Women: Struggling Against Deep-Seated Prejudices

Despite significant strides, women in India continue to grapple with deeply entrenched prejudices. Issues such as gender-based violence, workplace discrimination, and unequal access to opportunities persist. The struggle for women's rights intersects with broader societal challenges, including the need for attitudinal shifts and legal reforms.

2. Men: Breaking Free from Constricting Stereotypes

While traditional gender roles have predominantly favored men in certain aspects, they too face challenges arising from societal expectations. The pressure to conform to stoic masculinity, career-related stress, and limited emotional expression are some of the issues men grapple with. The evolving landscape calls for a reevaluation of what it means to be a man in contemporary India.

3. LGBTQ+ Community: Navigating a Heteronormative Terrain

The LGBTQ+ community in India faces unique challenges due to deeply ingrained heteronormativity. Discrimination, societal stigma, and legal hurdles create a complex environment for individuals who do not conform to traditional gender and sexual orientation norms. The fight for acceptance and equal rights is an ongoing struggle within the larger discourse on gender.

Conclusion

The journey into Indian mentality regarding gender roles is one marked by resilience, transformation, and ongoing struggles. While the traditional fabric of society continues to influence perceptions, the winds of change are undeniable. Education, economic empowerment, and societal awareness are reshaping the discourse, paving the way for a more inclusive and equitable future.

As we navigate this intricate landscape, it is crucial to recognize the agency of individuals in shaping their identities beyond the constraints of gender expectations. A holistic understanding of gender roles in India demands not only an acknowledgment of historical roots but an active engagement with the evolving dynamics that propel society towards greater inclusivity and equality. In the tapestry of Indian mentality, the threads of gender are being rewoven, reflecting a narrative that is diverse, complex, and ever-changing.

Introduction

In the vast tapestry of Indian culture and society, one cannot ignore the intricate patterns woven by the caste system. A system deeply rooted in the historical context of the subcontinent, it has not only shaped the social hierarchy but continues to cast a long shadow over individual lives. This article embarks on a journey into the Indian mentality, examining the historical roots of the caste system and its contemporary impact on social structures and individual destinies.

Understanding the Historical Context

1. Origins of the Caste System

The origins of the caste system can be traced back to ancient India, with its roots embedded in religious texts like the Vedas. Initially, the caste system was a stratification based on one's occupation, with four primary varnas – Brahmins (priests and scholars), Kshatriyas (warriors and rulers), Vaishyas (merchants and farmers), and Shudras (laborers). Over time, this simplistic division metamorphosed into a complex social structure with numerous jatis or sub-castes, creating a hierarchy that defined not only one's profession but also social status and privileges.

2. Brahminical Influence and Social Stratification

The rise of Brahminical influence further solidified the caste system. The Brahmins, as the custodians of religious texts and rituals, played a pivotal role in shaping societal norms. This resulted in the entrenchment of social hierarchy, where the Brahmins occupied the topmost rung, enjoying privileges and power, while the Shudras found themselves relegated to the lowest echelons, often facing discrimination and exclusion.

3. Impact of Foreign Invasions and Rule

The caste system underwent further transformations during periods of foreign invasions and rule. The arrival of the Mughals and later, the British, brought new dynamics to the social fabric of India. While the Mughals were relatively tolerant of existing social structures, the British, with their administrative reforms, inadvertently institutionalized certain aspects of the caste system for their own administrative convenience. This laid the groundwork for the stratified social order that persists today.

Contemporary Impact on Social Structures

1. Persisting Social Hierarchies

Despite India's journey into modernity, the caste system's shadow looms large. Social hierarchies persist, affecting various aspects of life, from education and employment to marriage and politics. The idea of 'reservation' in educational institutions and government jobs, meant to uplift historically marginalized communities, reflects the ongoing impact of the caste system on social structures.

2. Economic Disparities

The caste system has also contributed to economic disparities. Certain castes, historically disadvantaged, find it challenging to break free from the shackles of poverty. The allocation of resources and opportunities often favors those belonging to higher castes, perpetuating a cycle of disadvantage for those at the bottom of the social hierarchy.

3. Political Landscape and Representation

The caste system continues to influence the political landscape of India. Political parties often mobilize support along caste lines, exploiting existing social divisions for electoral gains. This has implications for governance and policy-making, as the focus sometimes shifts from broader developmental issues to narrow caste-based interests.

Individual Lives: Stories of Struggle and Resilience

1. Educational Challenges

For many individuals, particularly those from lower castes, accessing quality education remains a significant challenge. Deep-seated prejudices can affect the learning environment, hindering the academic progress of students from marginalized communities. The reservation system, while designed to address these imbalances, is not without its controversies and debates.

2. Employment Discrimination

The job market in India is not immune to the influence of the caste system. Discrimination in employment, often subtle but pervasive, continues to limit opportunities for individuals from certain castes. Breaking free from these barriers requires not only skill and determination but also a transformation in societal attitudes and perceptions.

3. Social Stigma and Inter-Caste Marriages

Inter-caste marriages, though increasingly prevalent, still face resistance in many parts of the country. Social stigma attached to marrying outside one's caste can lead to familial and societal ostracization. While urbanization and education are gradually eroding these prejudices, the battle against deeply ingrained beliefs is an ongoing struggle for many individuals.

Conclusion

A journey into the Indian mentality inevitably involves grappling with the complexities of the caste system. The historical context provides insights into its evolution, while the contemporary impact underscores the need for societal introspection and reform. As India continues to navigate the currents of progress, addressing the deep-seated inequalities perpetuated by the caste system becomes crucial. Only through collective efforts, societal awareness, and inclusive policies can the nation hope to unravel the threads of this complex social fabric and forge a more egalitarian future for all its citizens.

Chapter 5. Religious Influence on Daily Life

Introduction

In the vast and diverse landscape of India, religion is not merely a set of beliefs; it is a way of life, a cultural ethos that weaves through the fabric of society. The influence of religion on daily life in India is profound and multifaceted. This article delves into the intricate tapestry of religious influence, exploring how it permeates various aspects of life, from the mundane to the profound.

Rituals

Rituals are the rhythmic heartbeat of religious practices in India. From the crack of dawn to the tranquil dusk, individuals engage in rituals that connect them to their spiritual roots. Morning prayers, an integral part of many households, set the tone for the day. The act of lighting incense, offering flowers, and chanting hymns creates a serene ambiance, fostering a spiritual connection before embarking on daily duties.

Mealtime rituals, too, hold a special place. The act of offering food to deities before partaking symbolizes gratitude and a recognition of the divine in everyday sustenance. This ritualistic approach to meals transforms the mundane into the sacred, emphasizing the sanctity of nourishment.

Festivals

Festivals in India are not just occasions for revelry; they are vibrant expressions of religious fervor. Diwali, the festival of lights, symbolizes the triumph of good over evil, and the lighting of lamps signifies the dispelling of darkness. Holi, the festival of colors, transcends physical boundaries and brings people together in a riot of hues, symbolizing the unity in diversity that is deeply rooted in the Indian ethos.

During festivals, the entire community comes alive with shared rituals, prayers, and festivities. The streets are adorned with colorful decorations, and the air is filled with the scent of incense and the sound of devotional music. Festivals serve as reminders of cultural identity and strengthen the communal bond, making religion an inseparable part of the collective consciousness.

Daily Practices

In India, religious influence is not confined to specific times or spaces; it seamlessly integrates into the rhythm of daily life. From the sacred thread worn by some Hindus to the auspicious markings on foreheads, the visual symbols of religious identity are worn with pride. The donning of traditional attire is not just a fashion choice; it is a conscious affirmation of cultural and religious roots.

Moreover, the practice of yoga and meditation, deeply rooted in ancient Indian philosophies, has gained global recognition. These practices not only promote physical well-being but also offer a spiritual dimension, connecting individuals to their inner selves and, by extension, to something larger than themselves.

Social Customs

Religious influence extends beyond individual practices to shape social customs and norms. Marriage ceremonies, for instance, are elaborate affairs marked by rituals and traditions that vary across communities. These ceremonies are not only a union of two individuals but also a merging of families, with religious rites playing a central role in sanctifying the bond.

Similarly, the concept of dharma, or righteous duty, is deeply ingrained in the Indian psyche. The adherence to social responsibilities and ethical conduct is often guided by religious principles, emphasizing the interconnectedness of personal conduct and spiritual well-being.

Education and Knowledge

Education in India has historically been intertwined with religious teachings. Ancient scriptures like the Vedas and Upanishads were not only repositories of spiritual wisdom but also fountains of knowledge encompassing various disciplines. The gurukul system, where students lived with their teachers to imbibe not just academic knowledge but also moral and spiritual values, exemplifies the holistic approach to education rooted in religious principles.

Even in contemporary times, many educational institutions in India maintain a focus on moral and ethical education alongside academic pursuits. The reverence for knowledge and the pursuit of wisdom are seen as integral to spiritual growth, reflecting the enduring influence of religion on the educational landscape.

Art and Culture

Religious influence in India finds rich expression in its art and culture. Classical dance forms like Bharatanatyam and Odissi often depict stories from mythology, serving as a means of both artistic expression and spiritual storytelling. Temples, with their intricate architecture and vibrant sculptures, are not just places of worship but also living museums that narrate tales of devotion and divine intervention.

Indian literature, too, is replete with religious themes. Epics like the Ramayana and Mahabharata are not just stories; they are moral and philosophical treatises that continue to shape the moral compass of millions. The arts, in their myriad forms, become a medium through which the divine is not only celebrated but also communicated to the masses.

Conclusion

In the journey into the Indian mentality, one cannot overlook the pervasive influence of religion on daily life. It is a force that transcends individual beliefs, permeating every aspect of existence. From the sacred rituals that frame the day to the grand celebrations of festivals, from the daily practices that embody spiritual principles to the social customs that define relationships, religion weaves a tapestry of faith that binds individuals to their cultural roots.

This influence is not stagnant but dynamic, adapting to the changing currents of time while retaining its essence. It is a source of strength and solace, a compass that guides individuals through the labyrinth of life. In understanding the profound impact of religion on daily life in India, one gains insight into the resilient spirit that continues to shape the nation's ethos, fostering a harmonious coexistence of the sacred and the secular.

Introduction

In the vast tapestry of Indian culture, the institution of marriage stands as a cornerstone, weaving together the threads of tradition, familial bonds, and societal expectations. This article delves into the intricate nuances surrounding marriage and matrimony in India, exploring the contrasting dynamics of arranged marriages, love marriages, and the evolving concepts of partnerships.

Arranged Marriages

Arranged marriages, deeply rooted in tradition, have been a defining feature of Indian society for centuries. Guided by the principles of familial compatibility, shared values, and social standing, the concept of arranged marriages encapsulates the collective mindset of the Indian community. Families play a pivotal role in orchestrating these unions, acting as intermediaries in the pursuit of social harmony and the preservation of cultural norms.

1. The Role of Families

Arranged marriages are often orchestrated by families who diligently scrutinize potential matches, considering factors such as caste, religion, socio-economic status, and family background. The emphasis on familial compatibility reflects the belief that a successful marriage extends beyond the individual, encompassing the harmony of two families.

2. Compatibility and Adjustment

In arranged marriages, couples embark on a journey of discovery post-wedding, learning to build a life together. The emphasis on compatibility and adjustment becomes paramount, as individuals strive to adapt to their partner's personality, preferences, and familial expectations. The success of these marriages is often measured by the ability to navigate these initial challenges and forge a lasting bond.

Love Marriages

In recent decades, the landscape of matrimony in India has witnessed a seismic shift with the rise of love marriages. Fueled by changing societal attitudes, increased exposure to the global culture, and the advent of technology, love marriages challenge the conventional norms, placing individual choice and romantic compatibility at the forefront.

1. Individual Autonomy

Love marriages represent a departure from the traditional hierarchical approach to marriage, placing individual autonomy and personal choice at the forefront. The decision to marry is driven by the mutual feelings and understanding between the individuals involved, fostering a sense of agency and independence in choosing a life partner.

2. Navigating Cultural Boundaries

Despite the increasing acceptance of love marriages, many couples find themselves navigating cultural boundaries and overcoming societal expectations. Inter-caste and inter-religious marriages, once considered taboo, are gradually becoming more prevalent, reflecting a growing acceptance of diverse relationships within Indian society.

Evolving Concepts of Partnerships

As India continues to embrace modernity, the concept of partnerships is evolving, transcending the dichotomy of arranged and love marriages. This paradigm shift is marked by a more inclusive approach, where individuals seek compatibility, shared values, and emotional resonance, regardless of the marriage's origin.

1. The Role of Communication

In contemporary Indian marriages, communication plays a pivotal role in fostering understanding and connection between partners. The evolving mentality emphasizes open dialogue, enabling couples to navigate challenges, express their needs, and build a strong foundation for their relationship.

2. Balancing Tradition and Modernity

Couples in modern Indian marriages often grapple with the delicate balance between tradition and modernity. While upholding cultural values, they also seek to create spaces for individual growth, pursuing careers, and embracing changing gender roles. This delicate equilibrium reflects the adaptability and resilience of Indian partnerships.

Challenges and Opportunities in the Modern Landscape

The evolving landscape of marriage in India is not without its challenges. While traditional norms may resist change, there is an increasing recognition of the need for flexibility and acceptance in the pursuit of harmonious partnerships. It is essential to acknowledge and address these challenges to foster a more inclusive and progressive approach to matrimony.

1. Breaking Gender Stereotypes

One of the challenges in the modern Indian mentality lies in breaking gender stereotypes that have long defined marital roles. As couples strive for equality and shared responsibilities, there is a gradual dismantling of traditional gender norms, paving the way for more balanced and fulfilling partnerships.

2. Navigating Inter-generational Expectations

The clash between inter-generational expectations and evolving mentalities can create tensions within families. Bridging the gap between traditional values and contemporary aspirations requires open communication and a gradual shift in societal attitudes, creating opportunities for understanding and acceptance.

Conclusion

Marriage and matrimony in India form a rich tapestry woven with threads of tradition, cultural nuances, and evolving mentalities. The journey from arranged marriages to love marriages and the emergence of modern partnerships reflects the dynamic nature of Indian society. As individuals navigate the complexities of matrimony, they are redefining the narrative, fostering relationships based on mutual respect, communication, and shared aspirations. This journey into Indian mentality offers a glimpse into the diverse and evolving landscape of marriage, encapsulating the essence of a society in constant flux yet rooted in its cultural heritage.

Chapter 7. The Role of Tradition in Personal
Choices

Introduction

A rich tapestry of cultural traditions weaves through the
diverse landscape of India, influencing every aspect of life.
This profound connection to tradition significantly impacts
personal choices, shaping the decisions individuals make
regarding marriage, lifestyle, and self-identity. In this
exploration, we delve into the intricate relationship between
tradition and personal decisions, unraveling the threads that
bind the Indian mentality.

The Influence of Tradition on Marriage

Marriage in India is not just a union of two individuals; it is
a merging of families, communities, and traditions.
Traditional values play a pivotal role in shaping the
expectations and norms surrounding marriage. Arranged
marriages, a longstanding tradition, are a testament to the
influence of familial and societal values. The emphasis on
compatibility, shared cultural background, and familial
approval underscores the significance of tradition in the
choice of life partners.

The institution of marriage in India is deeply rooted in
customs and rituals, each carrying its own symbolic
meaning. From elaborate wedding ceremonies to age-old
rituals, every step is a reflection of tradition. The
preference for arranged marriages is often seen as a
commitment to upholding cultural values and preserving
the sanctity of familial ties. Even in the face of changing
times, many individuals find solace in adhering to these

time-honored practices, perceiving them as a source of stability in an ever-evolving world.

Lifestyle Choices

The intersection of tradition and lifestyle choices creates a dynamic landscape where individuals navigate between modern aspirations and age-old values. While globalization has introduced a plethora of options, the impact of tradition is evident in the choices related to food, clothing, and daily rituals.

Dietary preferences, deeply rooted in cultural practices, showcase the amalgamation of tradition and modernity. The traditional Indian diet, rich in spices and diverse flavors, is not just a culinary choice but a reflection of cultural identity. Even as individuals experiment with international cuisines, the comfort and nostalgia associated with traditional dishes continue to hold a special place in the hearts and palates of many.

Clothing, another significant aspect of lifestyle, becomes a canvas where tradition is vividly painted. The vibrant array of traditional Indian attire reflects regional diversity and cultural heritage. The choice of clothing is often a statement of identity, with individuals proudly donning garments that connect them to their roots. The coexistence of traditional attire and contemporary fashion exemplifies the delicate balance between embracing modernity and preserving cultural identity.

Daily rituals and practices, deeply ingrained in tradition, shape the rhythm of life for many Indians. From morning prayers to festive celebrations, these rituals provide a sense of continuity and belonging. While the pace of life may have accelerated with technological advancements, the essence of tradition continues to guide individuals in their daily routines, offering a sense of grounding and purpose.

Self-Identity

The concept of self-identity in the Indian context is a complex interplay of tradition and individuality. The pressure to conform to societal expectations often coexists with the desire for personal autonomy and expression. Traditional roles and expectations, especially in the context of gender, can significantly influence how individuals perceive and construct their identities.

The role of tradition in shaping gender roles is a nuanced aspect of self-identity. While traditional norms may prescribe specific roles for men and women, there is a growing awareness and push for gender equality. The tension between tradition and progressive ideals becomes palpable as individuals navigate societal expectations while striving for personal fulfillment. The evolving narrative of self-identity in India reflects a delicate negotiation between tradition and individual agency.

The generational gap further adds complexity to the construction of self-identity. Younger generations, exposed to a globalized world and diverse perspectives, often grapple with reconciling traditional values passed down by their elders with their own evolving beliefs. The clash between generations becomes a crucible where individual identities are forged, shaped by the heat of tradition and the transformative fire of personal experiences.

Conclusion

A journey into the Indian mentality unveils a landscape where tradition and personal choices are intricately intertwined. The influence of tradition on decisions related to marriage, lifestyle, and self-identity is profound and enduring. As individuals navigate the crossroads of tradition and modernity, they carve out unique paths that reflect the richness of the Indian cultural tapestry.

In this exploration, we have witnessed the enduring power of tradition in shaping the choices individuals make. From the sacred vows of marriage to the daily rituals that punctuate life, tradition provides a roadmap that guides individuals through the complexities of existence. As the journey into the Indian mentality continues, the interplay between tradition and personal choices will undoubtedly remain a central theme, weaving a narrative that is both timeless and ever-evolving.

Introduction

In the diverse tapestry of India's cultural and societal landscape, the pursuit of education and career holds a paramount position. This article delves into the intricate nuances of the Indian approach to education and career choices, unraveling the cultural and societal threads that weave the fabric of professional success.

The Cultural Underpinnings of Indian Education

India's rich history and cultural heritage significantly influence its approach to education. The emphasis on education as a means of enlightenment, reflected in ancient texts like the Vedas, underscores the cultural reverence for learning. Traditionally, education in India was intertwined with spiritual growth, creating a holistic perspective that extended beyond the mere accumulation of knowledge.

The Academic Pressure Cooker

One cannot discuss the Indian education system without addressing the prevalent academic pressure. From an early age, students are immersed in a competitive environment where success is often equated with high grades. The fierce competition, fueled by a vast population and limited resources, creates an academic pressure cooker, leaving little room for exploration and self-discovery.

Career Choices: Tradition vs. Passion

The Indian mentality towards career choices is often characterized by a delicate balance between tradition and individual passion. Many Indian families hold onto time-honored professions, passing them down through generations. The prestige associated with certain careers, such as engineering or medicine, often influences the choices of young minds. However, a paradigm shift is underway as the newer generations increasingly prioritize personal passion and fulfillment over societal expectations.

The Engineering and Medical Predicament

Engineering and medical fields have long been the flag bearers of career success in India. However, the sheer volume of graduates in these disciplines has led to a saturation of the job market. Many find themselves grappling with the dissonance between societal expectations and the stark reality of limited opportunities. The pursuit of these traditional careers often becomes a path of least resistance rather than a conscious choice aligned with personal aspirations.

The Emergence of Non-Conventional Paths

In recent years, there has been a noticeable shift in the Indian mentality concerning career pursuits. Non-conventional fields like arts, entrepreneurship, and technology have gained traction. The success stories of individuals who dared to deviate from the norm have inspired a generation to explore diverse paths, challenging the stereotypical notion of a successful career.

The Role of Socioeconomic Factors

Socioeconomic factors play a pivotal role in shaping educational and career trajectories in India. Access to quality education, career guidance, and opportunities is not uniform across the diverse socioeconomic strata. The disparities widen the gap between those who can afford to pursue their passions and those constrained by circumstances to opt for more conventional, financially stable paths.

Professional Success and Societal Validation

In the Indian context, professional success is often intricately linked with societal validation. The pursuit of a successful career is not just a personal journey but a communal one. The approval of family, relatives, and the community at large becomes a driving force, adding a layer of complexity to an individual's professional aspirations.

The Toll on Mental Health

The relentless pursuit of academic and professional success takes a toll on mental health, a facet often overlooked in the grand narrative of achievement. The stigma surrounding mental health issues further exacerbates the problem. The pressure to meet societal expectations, coupled with the fear of failure, creates a breeding ground for stress, anxiety, and burnout.

Changing Dynamics in the Global Context

As India becomes an integral part of the global economy, the dynamics of education and career pursuits are evolving. The younger generation, exposed to a globalized world, is redefining success beyond conventional parameters. The allure of international opportunities and the exposure to diverse cultures are reshaping the Indian mentality towards education and career choices.

Conclusion

In navigating the complex interplay between tradition and modernity, the Indian mentality towards education and career pursuits is undergoing a transformation. While the echoes of tradition still resonate, a new narrative is emerging - one that celebrates individual passion, embraces diverse career choices, and acknowledges the importance of holistic well-being. Understanding this intricate tapestry requires a nuanced exploration of cultural, societal, and individual threads that together weave the fabric of education and career pursuits in the Indian context.

Chapter 9. Entrepreneurship and Business Culture

Introduction

India, with its rich tapestry of culture and tradition, has long been a breeding ground for entrepreneurial spirit. The confluence of historical influences, diverse demographics, and a dynamic business landscape has fostered a unique entrepreneurial environment. In this exploration, we delve into the essence of entrepreneurship in India, dissect the intricacies of business culture, and uncover the profound role of family in shaping and sustaining business enterprises.

The Entrepreneurial Spirit in India

India's entrepreneurial spirit is deeply rooted in its history, marked by the presence of successful traders and merchants dating back to ancient times. The concept of 'vyapar' or trade has been integral to Indian society, establishing a foundation for the entrepreneurial mindset. In recent decades, the spirit has not only endured but flourished, with a surge in startups and a growing appetite for risk-taking.

1. Historical Context

India's historical trade routes, such as the Silk Road, facilitated commerce and cultural exchange. The ancient trading communities, like the Marwaris and Gujaratis, built formidable business networks that spanned across regions and even international borders. Their legacy continues to inspire contemporary entrepreneurs, fostering a sense of resilience and resourcefulness.

2. Changing Dynamics

In the post-independence era, the Indian entrepreneurial landscape witnessed a paradigm shift. The economic liberalization of the 1990s dismantled many regulatory barriers, opening doors for innovation and competition. This transformation paved the way for a surge in startups, with young and dynamic entrepreneurs challenging conventional norms.

Business Culture in India

Navigating the business culture in India requires an understanding of its intricacies, where tradition and modernity often coexist. A myriad of factors, ranging from social hierarchies to diverse regional practices, shape the business culture, creating a dynamic and sometimes challenging environment for entrepreneurs.

1. Relationship Building

Business relationships in India often extend beyond the transactional. Personal connections and trust play a crucial role, with entrepreneurs investing time in building strong networks. The emphasis on relationships is reflected in the prevalence of long-term partnerships and the significance of word-of-mouth referrals in business circles.

2. Hierarchy and Respect

India's societal structure influences business dynamics, with a clear hierarchy often observed in corporate settings. Respect for elders and authority is deeply ingrained, impacting decision-making processes and communication styles. Entrepreneurs must navigate these hierarchies while fostering an inclusive and collaborative work environment.

3. Time and Patience

The concept of 'Indian Standard Time' reflects a more relaxed approach to punctuality. Patience is a virtue in Indian business culture, where negotiations may take time, and decisions are often reached after careful consideration. Entrepreneurs must adapt to this rhythm, recognizing that building trust and understanding may require a longer gestation period.

The Role of Family in Business Enterprises

Family has traditionally played a pivotal role in Indian society, and this extends seamlessly into the business sphere. Many successful Indian enterprises are family-owned, and the intertwining of familial ties with business decisions adds a unique layer to the entrepreneurial landscape.

1. Family Businesses

India boasts a significant number of family-owned businesses, ranging from small enterprises to large conglomerates. The Ambanis, Adanis, and Kirloskars are prime examples of families that have not only sustained their businesses across generations but have also contributed significantly to the nation's economy.

2. Succession Planning

Succession planning is the systematic process of identifying and developing individuals within an organization to ensure a smooth transition of key roles and responsibilities as leaders retire or move on.

In the Indian business context, succession planning is a meticulous process. The passing of the baton from one generation to the next involves not only transferring ownership but also ensuring a smooth transition of values and vision. The emphasis on maintaining family legacies often dictates strategic decisions and future planning.

3. Values and Ethics

Family businesses in India often operate on a strong foundation of values and ethics. The familial bond is considered a source of trust and integrity, fostering a sense of responsibility towards employees and the community. This unique blend of familial and business values contributes to the sustainability and resilience of these enterprises.

Challenges and Opportunities

While the entrepreneurial spirit in India is thriving, it is not without its challenges. Navigating a diverse and complex market, overcoming bureaucratic hurdles, and adapting to rapidly evolving technologies present hurdles for both budding and established entrepreneurs. However, these challenges also bring opportunities for innovation and growth.

1. Market Diversity

India's diverse demographics, languages, and cultural nuances create a complex market landscape. Entrepreneurs must tailor their strategies to resonate with the diverse preferences and needs of the population. Successful ventures often leverage cultural insights to create products and services that cater to specific regional or demographic demands.

2. Technological Innovation

The digital revolution has ushered in a new era of opportunities for Indian entrepreneurs. The widespread adoption of smartphones and internet connectivity has opened up avenues for e-commerce, fintech, and other tech-driven sectors. *Fintech*, short for financial technology, refers to innovative solutions and technologies that leverage digital advancements to enhance and streamline financial services, including banking, payments, investments, and insurance. Entrepreneurs embracing technological innovation are well-positioned to capitalize on the changing consumer landscape.

3. Government Initiatives

The Indian government has introduced various initiatives to promote entrepreneurship, such as 'Make in India' and 'Startup India'. These initiatives aim to create a conducive environment for business growth, offering incentives and support to startups. Entrepreneurs keen on navigating the Indian market should stay abreast of such policies to harness the benefits they offer.

Conclusion

In the journey into Indian mentality, the exploration of entrepreneurship and business culture unveils a dynamic landscape shaped by historical influences, cultural nuances, and a complex interplay of familial ties. The entrepreneurial spirit thrives against a backdrop of rich traditions, presenting both challenges and opportunities for those willing to embark on this rewarding journey. Understanding the depth of India's business culture, with its emphasis on relationships, respect, and family values, is crucial for entrepreneurs seeking success in this diverse and dynamic market. As India continues to evolve, the entrepreneurial spirit remains a driving force, propelling the nation towards innovation, growth, and economic prosperity.

Chapter 10. Media and Entertainment Preferences

Introduction

In the diverse tapestry of Indian culture, media and entertainment play a pivotal role in shaping societal norms, values, and individual preferences. Understanding the Indian mentality requires a comprehensive exploration of the myriad ways in which Indians engage with various forms of media and entertainment. This article delves into the complex dynamics of media consumption, the vast array of entertainment choices, and the enduring impact of Bollywood and regional cinema on the collective consciousness.

Media Consumption Patterns

Indian media consumption is a fascinating mosaic reflecting the cultural, linguistic, and socio-economic diversity of the nation. While television remains a prominent medium, especially in rural areas, the urban landscape has witnessed a paradigm shift with the advent of digital platforms. Streaming services have become a ubiquitous presence in urban households, offering a plethora of content spanning genres and languages.

1. Television Dominance

Television remains a steadfast companion in Indian households, catering to a broad spectrum of viewers. The popularity of soap operas, reality shows, and daily serials is indicative of the diverse taste of Indian audiences. The daily routine often revolves around prime-time television, creating a shared experience that transcends geographical boundaries.

2. Digital Onslaught

The rise of digital platforms has redefined how Indians consume media. The accessibility and affordability of smartphones have democratized content consumption, allowing individuals to curate their viewing experiences. OTT (Over-The-Top) platforms have gained immense popularity, offering a mix of international and regional content, thereby appealing to a broad demographic.

Entertainment Choices

Entertainment in India is not merely a means of leisure; it is a reflection of the cultural ethos and societal dynamics. From traditional art forms to contemporary digital content, the choices made by individuals provide insights into their preferences, aspirations, and affiliations.

1. Cinematic Extravaganza

Bollywood, often dubbed as the heart of Indian cinema, exerts a profound influence on the entertainment landscape. The industry's ability to seamlessly blend drama, music, and dance has made Bollywood a global phenomenon. Indian audiences, irrespective of language or region, find a sense of unity in the shared experience of watching a Bollywood blockbuster.

2. Regional Riches

Despite the pan-Indian appeal of Bollywood, regional cinema holds its ground with pride. Each state boasts a unique cinematic heritage, offering narratives rooted in local cultures and traditions. The popularity of regional films is not confined to their respective states; they are gaining recognition on a national and international stage, amplifying the diverse voices within the Indian film industry.

3. Small Screen Narratives

The popularity of television series, both national and regional, underscores the Indian penchant for serialized storytelling. The emotional connect fostered by long-running serials often transcends mere entertainment, creating a sense of familiarity and belonging. This is particularly evident in the way characters from popular TV shows become a part of everyday conversations.

Impact of Bollywood and Regional Cinema

The influence of Indian cinema, both Bollywood and regional, extends beyond the realms of entertainment. It permeates societal norms, influences fashion trends, and shapes perceptions on a myriad of issues.

1. Societal Reflection

Bollywood, as a microcosm of Indian society, mirrors the changing dynamics of relationships, cultural norms, and societal expectations. The portrayal of characters and storylines often reflects prevailing social issues, contributing to a collective dialogue on topics such as gender equality, caste discrimination, and communal harmony.

2. Fashion and Trends

The 'Bollywood effect' is not limited to the silver screen; it spills over into the realm of fashion and lifestyle. The influence of film stars on clothing trends, hairstyles, and even linguistic expressions is palpable. Iconic dialogues and fashion statements from films often become ingrained in popular culture, shaping the way individuals express themselves.

3. Cultural Representation

Regional cinema, on the other hand, serves as a powerful medium for the representation of diverse cultures within the vast tapestry of India. These films act as cultural ambassadors, introducing audiences to the nuances and traditions of different regions. The celebration of local languages and customs fosters a sense of pride and identity among viewers.

Conclusion

In the journey into the Indian mentality, understanding the intricate relationship between media, entertainment preferences, and societal impact is indispensable. The preferences for television, digital content, Bollywood, and regional cinema collectively contribute to the rich cultural mosaic that defines India. Media and entertainment, in their various forms, serve not only as a source of recreation but as a reflection of the collective consciousness, providing a lens through which one can navigate the complexities of the Indian psyche.

Chapter 11. Political Awareness and Civic Engagement

Introduction

The intricate fabric of Indian mentality is woven with threads of diverse cultures, traditions, and beliefs. In the grand tapestry of this nation, one cannot ignore the prominent role that political awareness and civic engagement play in shaping the collective consciousness of its people. This article delves into the analysis of political awareness among Indians, explores the dimensions of civic engagement, and examines the pervasive influence of politics on everyday life.

The Mosaic of Political Awareness

1. Historical Context

To comprehend the current state of political awareness in India, one must trace the historical roots embedded in the struggle for independence. The fervor of the freedom movement ignited a spark of political consciousness, leaving an indelible mark on the psyche of the Indian populace. The legacies of leaders like Mahatma Gandhi and Jawaharlal Nehru continue to echo in the collective memory, shaping the political awareness of successive generations.

2. Evolving Political Landscape

Over the years, India has witnessed a dynamic political landscape marked by a multitude of parties, ideologies, and socio-economic paradigms. The rise of regional political forces has added a nuanced dimension to the political discourse, reflecting the diverse aspirations of the nation. The awareness of political nuances has grown, with citizens becoming more discerning and vocal about their rights and expectations.

3. Media's Role in Shaping Awareness

In the contemporary era, the media serves as a powerful conduit for political information dissemination. The advent of digital platforms and social media has democratized access to information, allowing citizens to stay informed and engaged. However, the flip side is the challenge of navigating through misinformation, making media literacy a crucial aspect of political awareness.

Civic Engagement: A Participatory Democracy

1. Defining Civic Engagement

Civic engagement involves active participation and involvement of individuals in the social, political, and community affairs of their society, contributing to the collective decision-making process and promoting the well-being of the community.

Civic engagement is the lifeblood of a vibrant democracy, and India, as the world's largest democracy, is no exception. It encompasses a spectrum of activities through which citizens actively participate in the democratic process, including voting, community involvement, and advocacy for social causes. The level of civic engagement reflects the health of a democracy and its responsiveness to the needs of the people.

2. Electoral Participation

Voting is the bedrock of civic engagement, and India witnesses massive turnouts during elections. The diversity of the electorate, spanning urban and rural landscapes, adds complexity to the electoral dynamics. However, while high voter turnout is a positive indicator, the depth of political awareness among voters and the impact of identity politics are critical areas of analysis.

Identity politics refers to the political mobilization and advocacy based on the shared experiences and characteristics of a particular social group, such as race, gender, sexuality, or ethnicity. It involves the recognition and promotion of group-specific interests, often influencing political and social discourse.

3. Grassroots Activism

Beyond the ballot box, Indians engage in grassroots activism to address local issues. Non-governmental organizations (NGOs), community initiatives, and volunteer work play a pivotal role in shaping the socio-political landscape. The intersection of civic engagement and social causes highlights the proactive role citizens play in creating positive change at the grassroots level.

Politics in Everyday Life

1. Societal Perspectives

In the tapestry of Indian mentality, the influence of politics is omnipresent in everyday life. From family discussions to workplace conversations, political discourse permeates societal interactions. The diversity of opinions reflects the multiplicity of political ideologies, making India a vibrant crucible of democratic dialogue.

2. Socio-Economic Impacts

Government policies and political decisions have a direct impact on the socio-economic fabric of the nation. The implications of economic reforms, social welfare programs, and infrastructural developments resonate deeply in the lives of citizens. The intersection of politics and daily life is particularly evident in areas like education, healthcare, and employment opportunities.

3. Cultural Narratives

Politics and culture share an intricate relationship, with each influencing the other. The narratives woven by political leaders often intertwine with cultural identities, shaping the ethos of communities. The celebration of festivals, observance of traditions, and the preservation of heritage are imbued with political undertones, showcasing the fusion of politics and culture in the Indian mindset.

Conclusion

As we journey into the heart of Indian mentality, the tapestry reveals the intricate patterns of political awareness and civic engagement. From the historical echoes of independence to the pulsating dynamics of contemporary democracy, the evolution is marked by resilience and adaptability. The influence of politics in everyday life is a testament to the integral role it plays in shaping the collective consciousness of a nation that thrives on diversity and democratic ideals. In this ongoing journey, the threads of political awareness and civic engagement continue to weave a narrative that reflects the evolving spirit of India.

Introduction

In the vast and diverse landscape of Indian mentality, social expectations play a pivotal role in shaping relationships. As individuals traverse the intricate web of friendships, community involvement, and social networks, they encounter a plethora of norms and customs that define their connections with others. This journey into the heart of Indian mentality unveils a rich tapestry of social expectations that not only influence personal relationships but also contribute to the broader cultural fabric.

Foundations of Friendship

Friendships in India are often deeply rooted in shared values, cultural backgrounds, and common experiences. The societal expectation of friendship extends beyond mere companionship, emphasizing loyalty, trust, and mutual support. Friendships are seen as an essential support system, providing emotional sustenance and a sense of belonging.

In Indian society, the concept of friendship is multifaceted, with distinctions between childhood friends, college buddies, and work companions. The expectations associated with each category vary, reflecting the evolving nature of friendships over time. Traditional values, such as loyalty and commitment, are often emphasized, creating a strong foundation for enduring relationships.

Community Involvement

Community holds a special place in Indian mentality, and the expectations surrounding community involvement are deeply ingrained. Whether it's participating in religious festivals, volunteering for social causes, or engaging in local events, individuals are expected to contribute actively to the well-being of their communities.

The concept of "society first" is a prevalent theme, with societal expectations encouraging a sense of responsibility towards one's community. This involvement fosters a sense of unity and shared identity, reinforcing the notion that individuals are interconnected and interdependent.

Social Networks

In the digital age, social networks have expanded beyond the physical realm, encompassing virtual spaces where relationships are cultivated and maintained. The societal expectations surrounding online interactions in Indian mentality often mirror those in face-to-face encounters. Respect, courtesy, and maintaining cultural sensitivity are emphasized in the virtual domain.

Indian social networks, both online and offline, are characterized by the intricate interplay of familial, professional, and educational ties. The boundaries between personal and professional relationships are fluid, and individuals are often expected to navigate these dynamics with finesse. The importance of maintaining a positive online persona aligns with the broader cultural emphasis on reputation and social standing.

Intersecting Identities

As individuals navigate the landscape of social expectations, the intersectionality of identities comes to the forefront. Gender, caste, religion, and socioeconomic status often intersect, shaping the expectations placed on individuals in their relationships. The nuances of these intersections influence the dynamics of friendships, community involvement, and social networks.

For instance, gender roles may dictate specific expectations within friendships, with varying degrees of intimacy accepted between male and female friends. Similarly, community involvement may be influenced by caste dynamics, and social networks may be shaped by religious affiliations. Understanding and negotiating these intersecting identities is integral to building authentic and respectful relationships within the Indian context.

Challenges and Evolving Dynamics

While societal expectations provide a cultural framework for relationships, they also pose challenges. The pressure to conform to traditional norms can stifle individuality and limit the scope for unconventional connections. Balancing personal aspirations with societal expectations requires a delicate dance, as individuals strive to forge meaningful relationships without compromising their authenticity.

The evolving dynamics of Indian society, marked by globalization, urbanization, and changing demographics, contribute to a shifting landscape of social expectations. Younger generations often find themselves negotiating between traditional values and modern ideals, creating a space for redefining relationships in the context of contemporary India.

Navigating Conflict and Harmony

Conflicts arising from differing expectations are inevitable in any society, and India is no exception. Navigating these conflicts requires a nuanced understanding of cultural nuances and effective communication. Traditional conflict resolution mechanisms, rooted in principles of compromise and reconciliation, play a crucial role in maintaining harmony within relationships and communities.

Harmony, a deeply cherished value in Indian culture, is often prioritized over individual discord. The art of finding common ground, understanding diverse perspectives, and fostering empathy is central to resolving conflicts and sustaining relationships amidst the myriad social expectations.

The Role of Communication

Effective communication serves as the linchpin in the realm of social expectations and relationships. Open dialogue allows individuals to express their needs, boundaries, and aspirations, fostering understanding and mutual respect. The art of articulating one's expectations while remaining receptive to others' viewpoints is crucial in navigating the intricate tapestry of Indian mentality.

In a society where indirect communication is often favored, nuances, unspoken expectations, and cultural subtleties play a significant role in interpersonal interactions. Learning to decipher these cues and communicate effectively is an ongoing process that contributes to the resilience and depth of relationships.

Conclusion

A journey into Indian mentality reveals a complex and nuanced landscape of social expectations that shape the intricate dance of relationships. From the foundations of friendship to community involvement and the expansive realm of social networks, individuals find themselves navigating a rich tapestry woven with tradition, culture, and evolving dynamics.

As India continues to evolve in the 21st century, the interplay between societal expectations and individual aspirations becomes increasingly significant. Balancing tradition with modernity, navigating intersecting identities, and fostering effective communication are essential aspects of cultivating meaningful relationships within the Indian context. In this journey, individuals discover not only the beauty of diverse relationships but also the resilience of the cultural fabric that binds them together.

Chapter 13. Modernization and Globalization

Introduction

In the vast tapestry of Indian culture and society, the threads of modernization and globalization have woven themselves intricately over the years. This article delves into the profound impact of these global forces on traditional Indian values and the collective mindset. As the world becomes increasingly interconnected, India finds itself at the crossroads of tradition and progress, negotiating the delicate balance between the old and the new.

The Evolution of Traditional Values

To understand the impact of modernization and globalization on the Indian mentality, it is crucial to trace the evolution of traditional values. India, with its rich history and diverse cultural heritage, has long been characterized by a deep-rooted sense of community, spirituality, and familial bonds. These values have been the bedrock of Indian society for centuries, shaping the way people live, interact, and perceive the world around them.

Modernization: A Catalyst for Change

Modernization, propelled by technological advancements and socio-economic shifts, has ushered in a wave of change across India. The advent of urbanization, industrialization, and the rise of a tech-savvy middle class have disrupted traditional norms and ways of life. Cities have become bustling hubs of innovation, commerce, and cultural exchange, challenging the age-old structures that once defined the Indian society.

Globalization: Breaking Down Borders

Globalization, on the other hand, has erased geographical boundaries and brought the world closer together. The influx of foreign ideas, products, and lifestyles has penetrated the Indian consciousness, creating a melting pot of cultures. The once insular Indian mindset is now exposed to a plethora of influences from across the globe, leading to a reevaluation of traditional values in the light of this globalized perspective.

The Impact on Family Dynamics

One of the most significant areas where modernization and globalization intersect with traditional Indian values is in the realm of family dynamics. The joint family system, once the cornerstone of Indian households, is undergoing a transformation. As urbanization spreads, nuclear families become more prevalent, challenging the traditional extended family structure. This shift has implications for the support systems and interdependence that were intrinsic to the Indian way of life.

Changing Gender Roles

The evolution of gender roles is another focal point of the clash between tradition and modernity. While traditional Indian society has been patriarchal, modernization has brought about a gradual shift towards more egalitarian gender roles. Globalization, through exposure to diverse cultural norms, has catalyzed conversations around gender equality, challenging deeply ingrained stereotypes and fostering a more inclusive mindset.

Education and Career Choices

The traditional emphasis on professions like medicine, engineering, and civil services is now being challenged by the changing landscape of education and career choices. With the global job market demanding diverse skill sets, young Indians are increasingly opting for unconventional careers in technology, arts, and entrepreneurship. This shift reflects the influence of a globalized economy on individual aspirations, challenging the traditional notions of success and prestige.

Religion and Spirituality

The impact of modernization and globalization on religion and spirituality is a nuanced exploration. While traditional religious practices continue to hold sway in many parts of India, there is an evident shift towards a more cosmopolitan spirituality. Cosmopolitan spirituality refers to a global and inclusive approach to spiritual beliefs and practices that transcend cultural, religious, or geographical boundaries. It emphasizes interconnectedness, unity, and a shared sense of humanity, encouraging individuals to draw inspiration from diverse spiritual traditions and perspectives. Globalization has exposed Indians to a variety of religious beliefs, practices, and ideologies, contributing to a more pluralistic and tolerant outlook.

Cultural Homogenization vs. Diversity

The globalized exchange of ideas and cultural influences has led to a paradoxical situation – on one hand, there is a fear of cultural homogenization as Western ideals permeate Indian society, and on the other hand, there is an embracing of diversity as Indians integrate global elements into their own cultural tapestry. This tension highlights the ongoing negotiation between preserving cultural identity and adapting to the changing global landscape.

Challenges and Opportunities

The collision of tradition and modernity has not been without its challenges. The rapid pace of change has led to a generation gap, with younger Indians embracing modern values while encountering resistance from the older generation holding on to tradition. Striking a balance between preserving cultural heritage and embracing progress is a delicate task, and India faces the challenge of navigating these complexities.

However, amidst the challenges, there are also opportunities for growth and synergy. India has the chance to leverage its traditional values of community, resilience, and adaptability to navigate the complexities of modernization and globalization. The integration of traditional wisdom with contemporary knowledge can create a unique Indian identity that is both rooted and forward-looking.

Conclusion

As we embark on a journey into the Indian mentality in the era of modernization and globalization, it becomes evident that the impact is profound and multifaceted. The interplay of tradition and progress, of old values and new ideas, defines the complex narrative of India's cultural evolution. In this intricate dance, India seeks to preserve its essence while embracing the opportunities that come with a globalized world. The journey into the Indian mentality is not just a reflection on the past but a dynamic exploration of the path forward, where tradition and modernity coexist in a delicate yet vibrant equilibrium.

Introduction

In the kaleidoscope of human consciousness, India stands as a beacon of spiritual wisdom and mindfulness practices. Rooted in ancient traditions, the Indian mentality has long been intertwined with a profound understanding of the self and the universe. This article embarks on a journey into the depths of Indian spirituality, shedding light on meditation practices, the transformative power of yoga, and the ceaseless quest for inner peace.

Understanding Spirituality in the Indian Context

1. Spirituality as a Way of Life

In India, spirituality is not confined to religious rituals; rather, it permeates every aspect of daily life. It is an all-encompassing approach that seeks to harmonize the mind, body, and spirit. This holistic perspective views the material and spiritual realms as interconnected facets of existence.

2. The Concept of Atman and Brahman

Central to Indian spirituality is the concept of 'Atman' – the individual soul – and 'Brahman' – the universal soul. The realization of the oneness between Atman and Brahman is considered the pinnacle of spiritual awakening. This profound insight forms the bedrock of various spiritual practices in India.

Meditation Practices

1. Vipassana Meditation

Vipassana, meaning 'clear seeing' or 'insight,' is a meditation technique that traces its roots to ancient India. Emphasizing mindfulness and self-awareness, Vipassana aims to penetrate the layers of illusion and ignorance, leading practitioners towards a direct experience of reality. This technique has gained global recognition for its transformative impact on the mind.

2. Transcendental Meditation (TM)

Transcendental Meditation, introduced by Maharishi Mahesh Yogi, is a widely practiced form of mantra meditation. With its origins in Vedic traditions, TM involves the repetition of a specific mantra to facilitate a state of deep restful awareness. Many individuals around the world have attested to the calming and centering effects of this meditation technique.

Yoga and the Union of Mind and Body

1. The Eight Limbs of Yoga

Yoga, often perceived in the modern world as a series of physical postures, extends far beyond its outward manifestations. Rooted in the ancient wisdom of India, yoga is a comprehensive system that guides individuals on a journey towards self-realization and spiritual growth. The foundational text outlining this path is the Yoga Sutras of Patanjali, which delineates the Eight Limbs of Yoga – a roadmap for achieving harmony between the mind, body, and spirit.

Yama – Ethical Guidelines

The first limb, Yama, lays the foundation for ethical living. It consists of five principles that serve as guidelines for social and moral conduct. These include Ahimsa (non-violence), Satya (truthfulness), Asteya (non-stealing), Brahmacharya (moderation or celibacy), and Aparigraha (non-possessiveness). By adhering to these principles, individuals cultivate a foundation of integrity and compassion in their interactions with the world.

Niyama – Personal Observances

Niyama, the second limb, focuses on personal observances and self-discipline. It comprises five principles: Saucha (cleanliness), Santosha (contentment), Tapas (discipline), Svadhyaya (self-study), and Ishvara Pranidhana (surrender to the divine). Niyama encourages individuals to cultivate inner strength, self-reflection, and devotion, creating a conducive environment for spiritual growth.

Asana – Physical Postures

Asana, perhaps the most well-known limb in the West, refers to the practice of physical postures. Beyond the aesthetic appeal, asanas are designed to prepare the body for meditation by promoting strength, flexibility, and balance. The postures are not an end in themselves but rather a means to attain physical well-being, mental clarity, and spiritual awareness.

Pranayama – Breath Control

The fourth limb, Pranayama, centers on breath control. Prana, often translated as life force, is harnessed through various breathing techniques to regulate the flow of energy in the body. By mastering the breath, practitioners cultivate a heightened sense of awareness, promote relaxation, and prepare the mind for meditation.

Pratyahara – Withdrawal of the Senses

Pratyahara involves withdrawing the senses from external stimuli and turning attention inward. In the modern era, bombarded by a constant influx of information, this limb is particularly relevant. By consciously redirecting attention from the external world to the inner self, individuals lay the groundwork for deeper concentration and meditation.

Dharana – Concentration

Dharana, the sixth limb, is the practice of concentration. It involves focusing the mind on a single point, object, or thought. Through unwavering concentration, practitioners begin to still the fluctuations of the mind, paving the way for the deeper states of meditation that follow.

Dhyana – Meditation

Dhyana, often synonymous with meditation, is the seventh limb. While Dharana is the focused concentration on a single point, Dhyana is the effortless flow of attention towards a chosen point of focus. In this state, the meditator experiences a profound sense of unity, transcending the duality of self and object.

Samadhi – Union with the Divine

The eighth limb, Samadhi, represents the ultimate goal of yoga – union with the divine. It is a state of profound bliss, where the individual transcends the ego and experiences oneness with the universal consciousness. Samadhi is not an endpoint but a continuous, evolving state of spiritual realization.

Each limb of yoga is intricately connected, forming a holistic path to spiritual awakening. The Eight Limbs provide a framework for individuals to navigate the complexities of the mind and cultivate a balanced, harmonious life. While the physical aspect of yoga is a gateway for many, the deeper transformative journey unfolds as practitioners progress through these limbs, ultimately leading to the realization of the self's interconnectedness with the vast expanse of the universe.

2. Hatha Yoga

Hatha Yoga, rooted in ancient wisdom, emerges as a holistic approach to well-being by intertwining physical postures and breath control. Central to this practice are the asanas, designed not only for physical strength and flexibility but also to stimulate energy centers within the body. The regulation of breath, or pranayama, serves as a bridge connecting the physical and mental realms. Hatha Yoga's focus on balancing energy channels and purification practices fosters a harmonious flow of vital energy, preparing the practitioner for deeper states of meditation.

This adaptable and accessible form of yoga places a profound emphasis on the mind-body connection, transforming the physical practice into a moving meditation. Through Hatha Yoga, individuals embark on a journey of self-discovery, unraveling the layers of tension in both body and mind, ultimately realizing the profound interconnectedness of their being.

The Quest for Inner Peace

1. Journey Inward: The Search for Self

Indian spirituality encourages individuals to turn their gaze inward, embarking on a profound journey of self-discovery. The idea is to explore the depths of one's consciousness, unraveling the layers of conditioning and ego that obstruct the realization of one's true nature.

2. Detachment and Non-Attachment

A recurring theme in Indian spirituality is the practice of detachment and non-attachment. This doesn't imply a rejection of the material world but rather a perspective that allows one to engage with life without being consumed by desires and attachments. The art of living with equanimity in the face of pleasure and pain is considered essential on the path to inner peace.

3. Karma Yoga

The Bhagavad Gita, a sacred text in Indian philosophy, expounds the concept of Karma Yoga – the path of selfless action. This philosophy advocates performing one's duties without attachment to the fruits of actions, emphasizing the idea that true fulfillment comes from the quality of one's actions rather than the outcomes.

Mindfulness in Everyday Life

1. Mindful Living

Mindfulness is deeply ingrained in the fabric of Indian mentality. From the practice of mindful eating to the art of conscious breathing, everyday activities are approached with an awareness that transcends the mundane. This approach to life fosters a heightened sense of presence and an appreciation for the richness of each moment.

2. Challenges in Modern Times

In the fast-paced and technologically-driven landscape of modern times, individuals face a myriad of challenges that can impact their mental well-being. The constant barrage of information, coupled with the demands of a competitive and interconnected world, often leads to stress, anxiety, and a sense of being overwhelmed. Incorporating mindfulness into everyday life has become increasingly crucial as a coping mechanism. However, the challenge lies in cultivating and sustaining mindfulness amidst the distractions and pressures of contemporary living. Balancing work, technology use, and personal relationships while maintaining a mindful awareness requires intentional effort and discipline. The ability to stay present, focused, and attuned to one's thoughts and emotions is an ongoing challenge, yet the rewards in terms of mental resilience and overall well-being make the pursuit of mindfulness in the face of modern challenges a worthwhile endeavor.

Conclusion

In the tapestry of Indian mentality, spirituality and mindfulness are threads woven seamlessly into the cultural and philosophical fabric. The journey inward, through meditation, yoga, and the pursuit of inner peace, reflects the timeless quest for understanding the self and its connection to the cosmos. As we delve into the rich spiritual landscape of India, we find not just practices but a way of life that beckons us towards a deeper, more meaningful existence.

Introduction

In the intricate tapestry of human existence, crises and challenges are inevitable threads that weave through the fabric of life. Exploring the Indian mentality in the context of these adversities reveals a fascinating interplay of cultural, historical, and societal factors. This article delves into the examination of how the Indian mentality copes with crises, challenges, and the resilience demonstrated in the face of adversity.

Understanding the Cultural Context

India, a land of diversity and ancient civilizations, boasts a rich cultural heritage that has shaped the mentality of its people. The concept of resilience is deeply ingrained in the cultural ethos, rooted in age-old philosophies like Vedanta and teachings from revered scriptures like the Bhagavad Gita. The belief in the cyclical nature of life and the impermanence of material existence provides a psychological foundation that aids in coping with crises.

Historical Perspectives

The annals of Indian history are marked by invasions, colonization, and socio-political upheavals. Despite facing centuries of external pressures, the Indian mentality has demonstrated remarkable resilience. The ability to absorb, adapt, and endure has been a hallmark of the Indian spirit. Whether it be the Mauryan Empire rebounding from the aftermath of the Kalinga War or the nation's emergence from colonial rule, history showcases instances of crisis turning into catalysts for resilience.

Spirituality and Resilience

Spirituality plays a pivotal role in shaping the Indian mentality's response to crises. The practice of yoga, meditation, and mindfulness has been integral to maintaining mental equilibrium during challenging times. The emphasis on detachment from material outcomes, as advocated in various spiritual traditions, contributes to a mindset that is less susceptible to the volatility of external circumstances.

Community and Social Fabric

The collectivist nature of Indian society provides a robust support system during times of crisis. The joint family system, prevalent in many parts of the country, serves as a safety net where the burden of challenges is shared among family members. The community, too, plays a vital role in fostering resilience. Festivals, rituals, and communal celebrations act as binding agents, nurturing a sense of belonging and solidarity that helps individuals weather the storms of life.

Economic Challenges and Adaptive Strategies

India's economic landscape has witnessed fluctuations, from periods of prosperity to economic downturns. The Indian mentality, marked by a frugal and resourceful approach, has often found innovative solutions to navigate economic challenges. Whether it be the informal sector's resilience in the face of job insecurity or the entrepreneurial spirit that flourishes in adversity, the economic aspect of the Indian mentality is a testament to the resilience ingrained in the culture.

Education and Learning

The Indian mentality places a high value on education, viewing it as a pathway to progress and prosperity. In times of crisis, the emphasis on learning becomes even more pronounced. Historical figures like Chanakya and contemporary icons like Dr. A. P. J. Abdul Kalam exemplify individuals who leveraged knowledge and wisdom to overcome challenges. The resilience of the Indian mentality is reflected in its commitment to continuous learning and intellectual growth.

Challenges in Governance and Political Resilience

The Indian political landscape has faced its share of challenges, from partition to emergency situations. The democratic system, though imperfect, has shown resilience in adapting to changing circumstances. Grassroots movements, citizen activism, and the ability to withstand political turbulence highlight the resilience embedded in the Indian mentality. The commitment to democratic values and the ability to participate in governance contribute to a collective resilience that transcends political uncertainties.

Crisis Response Mechanisms

The Indian mentality's response to crises involves a blend of pragmatism, spirituality, and community engagement. From the local self-help groups addressing societal issues to the numerous NGOs working on diverse challenges, there is a concerted effort to mitigate the impact of crises. The traditional practice of 'Satsang' or gathering for truth has evolved into contemporary forums for discussion and support, fostering a sense of resilience within communities.

Globalization and Changing Dynamics

In the era of globalization, the Indian mentality faces new challenges and opportunities. The ability to adapt to a rapidly changing world while retaining cultural roots requires a delicate balance. The resilience of the Indian mentality is evident in the diaspora's success stories, where individuals navigate diverse cultural landscapes without losing their core identity.

The term "*diaspora*" refers to the dispersion of a population outside its original homeland, and in this context, it pertains to individuals of Indian origin living in various parts of the world. The resilience of the Indian mentality is evident in how these individuals successfully navigate diverse cultural landscapes without compromising their core identity. Despite facing the challenges of assimilating into new societies, adapting to different cultural norms, and often encountering prejudices, members of the Indian diaspora manage to preserve and celebrate their unique identity, values, and traditions.

This ability to maintain a strong sense of self while embracing the complexities of multicultural environments reflects the resilience and adaptability ingrained in the Indian mindset, contributing to the success and positive integration of the diaspora on a global scale. The synthesis of tradition and modernity showcases an adaptive resilience that characterizes the Indian mindset on a global stage.

Conclusion

A journey into the Indian mentality in the context of crises and resilience reveals a nuanced interplay of cultural, historical, and societal factors. From the spiritual foundations that provide solace to the community bonds that offer support, the Indian mentality has weathered diverse challenges throughout history. Whether facing economic uncertainties, political upheavals, or the complexities of globalization, the resilience embedded in the Indian mindset remains a source of inspiration. As the world continues to evolve, understanding and appreciating the dynamics of crisis and resilience in the Indian mentality becomes imperative for fostering a global perspective on human endurance and adaptability.

Introduction

The dynamism of Indian society has been a subject of fascination for scholars and observers alike. Embedded in a rich tapestry of tradition and culture, India is witnessing a profound transformation in the mindset of its younger generations. This shift, characterized by a departure from conventional values, has sparked a debate on the evolving nature of the Indian mentality. In this article, we will delve into the intricate interplay of generational shifts and changing values, exploring how the youth in India are redefining societal norms and embracing more progressive perspectives.

Traditional Values in Flux

For centuries, India has been deeply rooted in its cultural heritage, guided by traditions and values that have stood the test of time. However, the advent of globalization and the rapid influx of information through digital channels have exposed the younger generation to a myriad of ideas and lifestyles. As a result, traditional values are now in a state of flux, with the youth questioning age-old norms and seeking a more inclusive, modern outlook.

Impact of Globalization

The globalization wave has swept across the Indian subcontinent, bringing with it a fusion of cultures and ideas. Young Indians, connected to the world through the internet and social media, are exposed to diverse perspectives that challenge the conservative ethos of the past. This exposure has catalyzed a shift towards more open-minded and cosmopolitan values (an outlook that embraces global interconnectedness, diversity, and the recognition of shared human experiences and responsibilities), eroding the barriers that once defined societal roles and expectations.

Changing Dynamics of Family Structure

The traditional joint family system, a cornerstone of Indian society, is undergoing a transformation as nuclear families become more prevalent. This shift in family dynamics is influencing individual aspirations and decision-making processes. Youngsters are no longer bound by the rigid hierarchies of the joint family, allowing them greater autonomy to shape their own destinies and challenge societal norms that may have been unquestioned in the past.

Education and Empowerment

Education has emerged as a powerful catalyst for change, empowering the youth with knowledge and critical thinking skills. As more young Indians pursue higher education and engage in intellectual discourse, they are challenging traditional norms that may perpetuate inequality or discrimination. This empowerment is not just limited to academic pursuits; it extends to social and cultural realms, fostering a generation that questions and seeks to rectify ingrained biases.

Gender Roles and Equality

One of the most notable aspects of generational shifts in India is the changing perspective on gender roles. Youngsters are increasingly challenging traditional gender norms and advocating for equality. The rise of the feminist movement, coupled with increased awareness of LGBTQ+ rights, is reshaping societal attitudes towards gender, pushing the boundaries of acceptance and understanding.

Technology and Social Media

The digital revolution has played a pivotal role in shaping the mindset of the younger generation. Social media platforms have become arenas for expressing individuality, sharing diverse opinions, and challenging societal norms. The democratization of information has given a voice to the youth, enabling them to mobilize and create collective movements that question the status quo.

Pursuit of Individualism

The younger generation in India is embracing individualism, prioritizing personal freedom and autonomy. This pursuit of individual identity often clashes with traditional values that emphasize collective well-being over personal aspirations. As the youth assert their independence, they are redefining success, relationships, and life goals in a manner that reflects their unique values and preferences.

Environmental Consciousness

An emerging trend among the younger generation in India is a heightened awareness of environmental issues. Concerns about climate change, pollution, and sustainability are shaping the values of the youth, prompting them to adopt eco-friendly lifestyles and advocate for policies that prioritize environmental conservation. This shift reflects a departure from purely economic pursuits to a more holistic and responsible approach to development.

Conclusion

The evolving mentality of the younger generation in India is a testament to the nation's ability to adapt and embrace change. Generational shifts and changing values are intrinsic to the growth and progress of any society, and India is no exception. As the youth challenge traditional norms, they are not discarding their cultural heritage but rather reinterpreting it in the context of a rapidly changing world. The journey into the Indian mentality is an exploration of resilience, adaptability, and the continuous evolution of a society that values its past while embracing the opportunities of the future.

In the vast tapestry of India's rich cultural heritage, societal norms, and historical intricacies, the evolution of the Indian mentality stands as a dynamic phenomenon. As we stand at the threshold of the future, poised on the edge of unprecedented social, economic, and technological changes, it is intriguing to contemplate how the collective mindset of India might transform. This chapter ventures into the realms of speculation, offering insights into potential shifts, challenges, and opportunities that could shape the future of Indian mentality.

Redefining Traditions in the Digital Age

As India embraces the digital revolution, traditional values and practices are bound to undergo a transformation. The younger generation, immersed in technology from an early age, is likely to reinterpret and redefine cultural norms. The internet, social media, and global connectivity will play pivotal roles in influencing perspectives, breaking geographical barriers, and fostering a more cosmopolitan worldview.

The Erosion of Caste Barriers

The age-old caste system, deeply rooted in historical stratifications, may witness a gradual erosion. Education, urbanization, and increased social mobility are likely to break down traditional barriers, fostering a society that values merit over birthright. The younger generation, exposed to diverse influences, might be more inclined to forge connections based on shared interests and talents rather than adhering strictly to caste affiliations.

Empowering Gender Equality

The discourse on gender roles and expectations is poised for a paradigm shift. Ongoing efforts to empower women, coupled with increased awareness and education, may result in a more equitable society. Women, armed with education and opportunities, might redefine their roles in both familial and professional spheres, challenging traditional norms and fostering a more inclusive environment.

Globalization and Cultural Synthesis

As globalization continues to weave its intricate threads into the fabric of Indian society, a cultural synthesis is likely to occur. The fusion of traditional values with global perspectives may create a unique blend that defines the Indian mentality of the future. This synthesis could manifest in diverse areas, from fashion and cuisine to entertainment and lifestyle choices, showcasing a harmonious coexistence of tradition and modernity.

Education as a Catalyst for Change

The chapter on Education and Career Pursuits emphasized the significance of education in shaping the Indian mindset. In the future, a more dynamic and progressive education system may emerge, encouraging critical thinking, creativity, and a broader understanding of global issues. This, in turn, could produce a generation of individuals with a more open-minded approach to problem-solving and decision-making.

The Evolving Notion of Success

Success, traditionally measured by academic and professional achievements, might undergo a *metamorphosis* (profound and often marked transformation or change, typically in form or nature, undergoing a significant and fundamental alteration). The younger generation, driven by a desire for purpose and fulfillment, may redefine success to include factors such as personal happiness, social impact, and environmental sustainability. This shift could herald a more holistic approach to life and success.

Technological Integration and Social Connectivity

The ubiquity of technology is likely to redefine the way Indians connect and communicate. Virtual platforms and social media may become even more integral to daily life, influencing social interactions, relationships, and the exchange of ideas. The challenge will be to balance the advantages of technological integration with the preservation of meaningful face-to-face connections.

Sustainable Living and Environmental Consciousness

Concerns about climate change and environmental sustainability are gaining prominence globally, and India is no exception. The future Indian mentality may prioritize eco-friendly practices, sustainable living, and a heightened awareness of environmental issues. This shift could manifest in lifestyle choices, consumption patterns, and a collective commitment to preserving the country's natural resources.

Political Awareness and Civic Responsibility

The political landscape of India is evolving, with increased youth participation and awareness. The future might see a more politically engaged and socially responsible populace. Issues such as governance, transparency, and social justice could become central to the collective consciousness, shaping the way Indians participate in and contribute to the democratic process.

Spirituality in the Modern Context

While spirituality has been a cornerstone of the Indian mentality, its expression may evolve in the future. The integration of ancient wisdom with contemporary practices, including mindfulness, meditation, and holistic well-being, could become more prevalent. Individuals may seek spiritual fulfillment amidst the fast-paced, technology-driven modern life.

Adaptability and Resilience in the Face of Challenges

The chapter on Crisis and Resilience highlighted the innate ability of the Indian mentality to weather storms and emerge stronger. This resilience will continue to be a defining trait in the future, as Indians adapt to global changes, economic shifts, and unforeseen challenges. The capacity to navigate uncertainty and maintain a sense of community may be crucial in shaping the Indian mindset.

The Role of the Global Indian Diaspora

The vast Indian diaspora, dispersed across the globe, is actively contributing to the diversity of thought and experience. The interactions between the global Indian community and diverse cultures are likely to influence the evolution of the Indian mentality. This interplay could lead to a more interconnected and globally aware mindset.

Preserving Cultural Roots Amidst Change

As India hurtles towards the future, it becomes imperative to strike a balance between embracing change and preserving cultural roots. The challenge lies in fostering a sense of pride in cultural heritage while remaining receptive to progressive ideas and global influences. The ability to navigate this delicate equilibrium will shape the trajectory of the Indian mentality.

Conclusion: A Tapestry of Possibilities

The future of Indian mentality is a tapestry woven with threads of possibility, uncertainty, and potential. As the nation navigates the uncharted waters of the 21st century, the resilience, adaptability, and openness of the Indian mindset will be critical. The journey into the future is marked by the interplay of tradition and innovation, and only time will unveil the intricate patterns that emerge.

In concluding this book on "A Journey into Indian Mentality", it is evident that the Indian mindset is not static but a dynamic force, continuously shaped by the ebb and flow of societal, cultural, and global influences. The chapters have provided a glimpse into the multifaceted layers of the Indian mentality, offering insights into its complexities, strengths, and areas for growth. As we stand at the intersection of tradition and modernity, the future beckons with promises and challenges, inviting the people of India to embark on a journey of self-discovery and collective evolution.

Embark on a captivating exploration of the intricate tapestry that weaves the fabric of Indian mentality with the book "A Journey into Indian Mentality". In this enlightening literary voyage, the book unfolds its narrative through seventeen thought-provoking chapters. From the foundational 'Introduction to Indian Mentality', offering an overview of the cultural, historical, and societal factors shaping the Indian mindset, to the future-focused 'The Future of Indian Mentality', each chapter delves into a specific facet of this rich tapestry. Readers will traverse the complexities of family dynamics, gender roles, caste structures, religious influences, and the intertwining of tradition with personal choices.

The book navigates through the realms of education, career pursuits, entrepreneurship, media preferences, political awareness, social expectations, and the transformative impact of modernization and globalization. It also explores the spiritual dimensions of Indian life, resilience in times of crisis, and the evolving values across generations. With insightful analysis and a forward-looking perspective, "A Journey into Indian Mentality" promises an engaging odyssey through the diverse layers that define the Indian psyche.

ABOUT THE AUTHOR

Mr. C. P. Kumar is a retired Scientist 'G' from National Institute of Hydrology, Roorkee, Uttarakhand, India. He is also a Reiki Healer and Chakra Balancing practitioner (with pendulum dowsing) and offers Emotional Freedom Technique (EFT) to help individuals with emotional issues. Mr. Kumar has authored many books on technical, spiritual, and social topics.

For further details, you may visit his webpage
https://www.angelfire.com/nh/cpkumar/virgo.html